I Can Do Lots of Stuff!

By Samantha Rabe

Illustrated by Aleksey Ivanov

Target Skill Cause and Effect

PEARSON

Scott
Foresman

I am five.

Kris and Brad are three.

See me skip!

Kris can not skip yet.

Look at me flip!

Kris can not flip yet.

See me fix the truck!

Brad can not fix it yet.

Look at me snap my fingers!
Brad can not snap
his fingers yet.

See me fill a glass!

I can get snacks for us.

I am five. I am big.
I can do lots of stuff!